Creation Groans On

Creation Groans On

Nature Images

KEN BAZYN

RESOURCE *Publications* • Eugene, Oregon

CREATION GROANS ON
Nature Images

Copyright © 2021 Ken Bazyn. All rights reserved. Except for brief quotations in critical publications or reviews, no part of this book may be reproduced in any manner without prior written permission from the publisher. Write: Permissions, Wipf and Stock Publishers, 199 W. 8th Ave., Suite 3, Eugene, OR 97401.

Resource Publications
An Imprint of Wipf and Stock Publishers
199 W. 8th Ave., Suite 3
Eugene, OR 97401

www.wipfandstock.com

PAPERBACK ISBN: 978-1-7252-9463-9
HARDCOVER ISBN: 978-1-7252-9464-6
EBOOK ISBN: 978-1-7252-9465-3

03/04/21

New Revised Standard Version Bible, copyright 1989, Division of Christian Education of the National Council of Churches of Christ in the United States of America. Used by permission. All rights reserved.

Contents

Acknowledgments	ix
Introduction: Jesus, the Lion of Judah	xi
The Spring Rain	2
Sleep Comes Gently	5
Late Winter's Thaw	8
The Rainy Season	11
Fog	14
To a Waterfall	17
Calling Upon the Wind	19
The Interminable Tedium of the High Plains	21
The Desert as City	23
The Shore	26
At the Beach	28
Breakers	30
Island Prisons	32
In the Turquoise Deserts of the Sea	35
Carefree	37
Upon Finding a Flower Blooming	39
The Lilies	41
Water-Lily Beauty	43
Tumbling Nests	45

Broadcast, Don't Drill	47
Bumper Ennui	50
The Dangling Tomatoes	53
Pumpkins and Gourds	55
Ungovernable Fingers	57
The Corn Palace	59
These Damnable Flies	61
The Prey	64
For Fluffy	66
The Animal Game	68
Breakthrough	71
Hope	73
Congratulatory Feedback	75
Noah and the Ark	77
An Imaginative Exercise for William James	80
The Flood of Time	82
A Utopian Solution	84
The World's the Bride	86
Thoughts of Human Grandeur	89
Creation Groans On	91
Bless the Lord	94
Chewable Spirituality	97
God Wants Only Lambs	99
A Morbid Autumn	101
Tumble-Down Crosses	103
I'll Be Transformed	105
Absolute Zero	108
Death like a Vine	110
Unbelief	112
The Hidden Things of God	114
Incalculable Things	117

Maya	120
Space . . .	122
The Shadow	125
Time, That Fleeting Deer	128
On Gathering Stars	130
Signs of the Zodiac	132
Song of a Shaman	134
How Do You Wake Up?	137
Sunset	139
Listing of Photographs	141
Works Cited	145

Acknowledgments

ONCE AGAIN I WANT to give credit to my wife, Barbara, for encouraging my poetry writing and for making all manner of corrections to improve their overall substance and style. David Reynolds, too, once more lent his expertise into making the work fit within Wipf & Stock's recommended parameters and pointing out assorted weaknesses.

I'm pleased that Wipf & Stock continues to be so committed to publishing top-notch religious poetry. Rachel Saunders displays fine-tuned typesetting talents throughout the book. My 35mm black-and-white shots were developed with care by Robert Meier, while Rockbrook Camera in Omaha turned the negatives into an easy-to-reproduce CD.

Introduction

Jesus, the Lion of Judah

THE BOOK OF JOB famously advises, "But ask the animals, and they will teach you" (12:7). Indeed, creation reveals the handiwork of the Lord (Rom. 1:20). Bonaventure argued that aspects of the physical world can be seen as "shadows, echoes and pictures, the vestiges, images and manifestations" of its creator.[1] "The immense magnificence of the visible world, its inconceivable vastness, the incomprehensible height of the heavens," writes American theologian Jonathan Edwards, "is but a type of the infinite magnificence, height and glory of . . . the spiritual world."[2] While the Bible is the written record of God's direct revelation through prophets, apostles, chroniclers, and so on, nature is often referred to as God's "second book."[3]

Homo sapiens are part and parcel of the animal kingdom. "At a single stroke," philosopher William James maintains, theism "changes the dead blank *it* of the world into a living *thou*, with whom the whole man may have dealings."[4] In *The Life of St. Francis*, Bonaventure relates how when Francis "considered the primordial source of all things, he was filled with even more abundant piety, calling creatures, no matter how small, by the name of brother or sister, because he knew they had the same source as himself."[5] Recall how God saved representative human beings and animals in the Ark. Following the Genesis flood, he made a covenant with Noah, urging all of life to be fruitful and multiply (Gen. 9:1–18)—indicating both

---

1. McGrath, *Theology: Basic Readings*, 51. Cf. Bonaventure, *Soul's Journey into God*, 75–78.
2. Smith, *Jonathan Edwards Reader*, 21.
3. Endicott, *Prose of Sir Thomas Browne*, 21.
4. James, *Will to Believe*, 127.
5. Bonaventure, *Soul's Journey into God*, 254–55.

INTRODUCTION

a love for biodiversity and life's interdependence.⁶ In John Wesley's sermon "The General Deliverance," he spoke of how the new heavens and the new earth would restore Paradise to all beings; thus we should "enlarge our hearts towards those poor creatures to reflect that, as vile as they appear in our eyes, not one of them is forgotten in the sight of our Father which is in heaven."⁷ "Each creature possesses its own particular goodness and perfection" which should be respected, asserts the *Catechism of the Catholic Church*; "no creature is self-sufficient."⁸ And Anglican bishop John Austin Baker wondered aloud whether we should humbly recognize that "other creatures have truths which we can only dimly grasp, worlds we can never fully enter."⁹

Calvin employed a cluster of metaphors to describe the "spectacle" of God's glory in nature. He spoke of the world as a "mirror" or "living likeness" of God. It is a "painting" whose strokes convey the divine splendor. It is a "spacious and splendid house," filled with abundant and exquisite furnishings. Contemplating heaven and earth is a school to educate God's children.¹⁰ "As soon as we acknowledge God to be the supreme architect, who has erected the beauteous fabric of the universe," Calvin stated, "our minds must necessarily be ravished with wonder at his infinite goodness, wisdom and power."¹¹ A similar feeling arose in the Counter-Reformation figure Ignatius of Loyola: "The greatest consolation he received was to look at the sky and the stars, which he often did and for a long time," Ignatius writes in the third person in his autobiography, "because as a result he felt within himself a very great desire to serve our Lord."¹²

Nature, too, played a key role in the conversion of twentieth-century Russian Orthodox theologian Sergius Bulgakov. At the age of twenty-four, he began to question his own philosophical skepticism. Suddenly "my soul was joyfully stirred," he declared. "I started to wonder what would happen if the cosmos were not a desert and its beauty not a mask or deception—if nature were not death, but life. If he existed, the merciful and loving Father,

---

6. Nash, *Loving Nature*, 101.

7. Nash, *Loving Nature*, 129. Cf. Outler, *Works of John Wesley, Vol. 2*, 449.

8. Catholic Church, *Catechism of the Catholic Church*, 88.

9. Baker, *Travels to Oudamovia*, 54. Cf. Linzey, *Animal Theology*, 47.

10. Lane, *Ravished by Beauty*, 59. Cf. McNeill, *Calvin: Institutes of Christian Religion, Vol. 1*, 51–66, 179–80.

11. Lane, *Ravished by Beauty*, 69.

12. Olin, *Autobiography of St. Ignatius Loyola*, 25.

Introduction

if nature was the vesture of his love and glory, and if the pious feelings of my childhood, when I used to live in his presence, when I loved him and trembled because I was weak, were true."[13]

We can appreciate the theological and spiritual significance of nature by, for example, focusing on one animal, the lion. In the Book of Revelation chapter five, Jesus is called "the Lion of the tribe of Judah" (5:5). This phrase can be traced back to that final blessing Jacob gave to his sons, when he compared Judah to a lion's whelp (Gen. 49:9). Lions later come to represent members of the royal household of Judah (Ezek. 19:2-9). On either side of Solomon's ivory throne were armrests with two sculpted lions; on either side of the steps leading up to the throne stood six additional lions (1 Kgs. 10:18-20). The messianic kingdom, according to the Book of Revelation, will be ruled by a hybrid beast resembling both a lion and a lamb. Jesus is obviously "the Lamb that was slaughtered" in 5:12, yet it was his lion-like nature which gave him the power to open the great scroll and break its seven seals in 5:5. This hybrid beast symbolizes not so much destruction as sacrifice and obedience.[14]

Let's discuss lions in general, then apply several of their major characteristics to Christ. They are commonly known as the "king of beasts." The lion's powerful body and large head (plus the long mane of the male) give it a majestic appearance. It can be nearly four feet tall and nine-and-a-half feet long, and weigh more than five hundred pounds; however, most are only two-thirds that size. The tail is half as long as the body and ends in a tuft on the male. Lions tend to be golden (or yellow-brown) with occasional patches of black, though the mane is usually a darker hue. They are full grown by the age of five or six and can live twenty to twenty-five years in captivity. Lions prefer to roam in the plains, scrub or thorn forests; there their tawny coats blend in better than in deserts or jungles.[15]

For a den, or lair, the lion chooses a well-hidden place. It may be a dense thicket, a patch of reeds, an outcropping of rocks covered by brush, or a cavern protected by thorns. A lioness can have up to six cubs in a litter, but more likely, she has two or three. Cubs are born with their eyes fully open. Early on, they are as playful and affectionate as kittens, but as they mature, they become too rough to handle. They learn to hunt when they are five or six months old, usually by trailing their mother, or less often, their

---

13. Bulgakov, *A Bulgakov Anthology*, 10-11.
14. Ryken, et al., "Lion," 514-15.
15. Cahalane, "Lion," 298-301.

Introduction

father. As a form of play, the cubs will wrestle, stalk, and pounce on each other—even nipping or slapping.[16] "To the thinking mind," eighteenth-century parson-naturalist Gilbert White contends, "nothing is more wonderful than that early instinct which impresses young animals with the notion of ... their natural weapons, and of using them properly in their own defense, even before those weapons subsist or are formed. Thus a young cock will spar at his adversary before his spurs are grown; and a calf or a lamb will push with their heads before their horns are sprouted."[17]

Typically lions sleep in their dens during the heat of the day or lounge under a shade tree, seeking out food chiefly at night or by twilight. They will hunt antelope, zebra, wild ass, warthog, and bush pig, as well as young rhinoceros, hippopotamus, elephant, and giraffe. Their front legs, approximately nineteen inches in circumference, are powerful; at the ends of their feet are sharp, horny claws. A lion kills small prey with a single blow, either by breaking the neck, or by tearing open the throat. The blow of the paws is said to have the force of a steam hammer. A lion brings down a large animal by first grasping the victim's nose with its huge paw, then jerking back on its head or hooking his forepaws on the rump, then knocking the animal off its feet. Sometimes it simply fastens its teeth on the throat.[18] It may wait in ambush near a water hole; like a domestic cat, it stalks its prey until it comes close enough to make a last-minute bounding rush. Lions have been known to spring more than twenty-one feet; this short burst is swift, but the lion cannot sustain such a speed for any great distance.[19]

Let me now enumerate three leonine characteristics of Christ. First is the animal's awesome strength and might. It is ferocious, taking prey at will. "The lion, which is mightiest among wild animals," claims Proverbs 30:30, "does not turn back before any." To be in the mouth of a lion is a dire predicament from which escape is nigh unto impossible. In an Aesop fable, an older lion has grown weak, so he pretends to be sick, sitting inside his cave, inviting other animals to come and pay their respects—whereupon he eats them. One day a fox decides to visit, but she greets him from outside the entrance. The lion asks why she won't come in. Her reply: "Because I see the tracks of those going in, but none coming out."[20] Or consider the plight

---

16. Schaller, *Golden Shadows, Flying Hooves*, 81, 86, 73–74.
17. White, *Natural History of Selborne*, 192.
18. Schaller, *Golden Shadows, Flying Hooves*, 146, 159.
19. Cahalane, "Lion," 298–301.
20. Aesop, *Aesop's Fables*, 12.

Introduction

of the Old Testament prophet Daniel. King Darius has him thrown into a den of lions (Dan. 6); he manages to survive only due to the intervention of an angel who stopped their mouths. The Cowardly Lion in *The Wizard of Oz* by L. Frank Baum rightly seems an anomaly, since he is eager to obtain courage, a quality that lions usually have in abundance.[21]

Before David did battle with the giant Goliath, he told King Saul how if a lion or bear had stolen a lamb from his father's flock, he would follow the predator, smite it, and pull the lamb out of its mouth. Ashurbanipal, inheriting the world's largest empire in 606 BC, ruled Assyria from its capital, Nineveh, where his might and power were depicted in a series of stunning reliefs on the North Palace (now in the British Museum), which display how he hunted lions while on horseback, on foot, and in a chariot, with assorted weapons. These images sought to raise the king's prestige in the eyes of all who beheld them.[22] In ancient Egypt the goddess Sekhmet was pictured as a lioness. Dressed in red (the color of blood), she protected the Pharaoh and led him into battle. Among the coins minted to honor the conquests of Alexander the Great, some show him with a hood consisting of the skin of a lion's head.[23] That English monarch who became known for his bravery during the Third Crusade was called Richard the Lion-heart. Christ as the lion-lamb in the Book of Revelation is ever victorious over formidable foes—a miracle-working beast, a false prophet, and that ancient serpent (or dragon), the devil (Rev. 13:11–18; 19:11—20:2). How appropriate then in Carl Jung's psychology that the lion stands for tremendous energy along with masterful self-control, the aggressor against whom all prove defenseless.[24]

A lion's roar can be heard for over two miles;[25] if you stand close by, it literally vibrates your body.[26] That sound can send entire villages into panic. In Hosea (11:10) and Joel (3:16), God himself is said to roar like a lion, shaking both the heavens and earth.[27] Drawing on this imagery, Matthew paints a portrait of Christ's second coming: "Immediately after the suffering of those days the sun will be darkened, and the moon will not give its

---

21. Baum, *Wizard of Oz*, 47–55.
22. Reade, "Assyrian Royal Hunt," 52–79.
23. Charbonneau-Lassay, *Bestiary of Christ*, 7–8.
24. Biedermann, *Dictionary of Symbolism*, 211.
25. Schaller, *Golden Shadows, Flying Hooves*, 94.
26. Hahn, *Learning from the Lizard*, 51.
27. Charbonneau-Lassay, *Bestiary of Christ*, 13.

INTRODUCTION

light; and the stars will fall from heaven, and the powers of heaven will be shaken. Then the sign of the Son of Man will appear in heaven, and then all the tribes of the earth will mourn, and they will see 'the Son of Man coming on the clouds of heaven' with power and great glory" (Matt. 24:29–30). I'm reminded of that modern folk song "The Lion Sleeps Tonight," originally recorded by the South African singer Solomon Linda and released in 1939. Linda was experimentally howling and yodeling in the studio, until on the third take, he improvised that captivating melody which has made the piece a bestseller worldwide: "Hush, my darling, don't fear, my darling/ The lion sleeps tonight."

Lions, too, like Jesus, came to stand for justice. A quite different Aesop fable tells of a beloved lion-king, before whom "all the wild animals assembled to present their petitions and receive verdicts in their disputes. Every animal was called to account: the wolf for what he had done to the lamb, the leopard for what she had done to the wild goat, the tiger for what he had done to the deer, and so on." Thus did the timid hare rejoice, "Now has come the day for which I have always prayed, when even the weak creatures are feared by the strong!"[28] In the middle ages ecclesiastical justice was frequently administered in the forecourts of churches, at a portal framed by stone lions; there the verdicts were handed down, appropriately enough, *inter leones et coram populo* ("between the lions and before the assembled people").[29]

Another way in which lions are like Christ is how they hunt. The lion is stealthy, difficult to detect, virtually noiseless. A famous Carl Sandburg poem begins, "The fog comes/on little cat feet."[30] Luther refers to deity as *Deus absconditus*, "the hidden God." This is a term borrowed from Isaiah 45:15 to indicate that knowledge of God can only come through God's self-revelation, since he is hid from human reason due to sin and death.[31] Christ, in Colossians, is declared to be the exact likeness of God, who is invisible (1:15). Though Jesus was in the world, and the world was made through him, the world knew him not, insists John's Gospel (1:10). Even when Jesus healed, he could sternly order the witnesses not to let anyone know (Luke 8:56).

Day in and day out God goes about his work unobtrusively. Like a lion, he creeps up behind us unawares, pounces, overthrowing our hearts.

28. Aesop, *Aesop's Fables*, 14.
29. Charbonneau-Lassay, *Bestiary of Christ*, 9.
30. Sandburg, "Fog," *Harvest Poems: 1910–1960*, 39.
31. McKim, *Westminster Dictionary of Theological Terms*, 86.

Introduction

He nudges, tugs at our sympathies, redirects, converts us. "The wind blows where it chooses, and you hear the sound of it, but you do not know where it comes from or where it goes. So it is with everyone who is born of the Spirit," Jesus made clear to Nicodemus (John 3:8). In G.K. Chesterton's "The Queer Feet," the famous detective Father Brown rescues the valuable knives and forks stolen from that exclusive dining club known as "The Twelve True Fishermen." The thief, he explains to the members, had repented. One asks, "Did you catch this man?" Brown replies, "Yes, I caught him with an unseen hook and an invisible line which is long enough to let him wander to the ends of the world, and still to bring him back with a twitch upon the thread."[32]

In Victorian England, Charles Spurgeon was the pastor-evangelist of the six-thousand-seat Metropolitan Tabernacle in London, the largest congregation in the world. His sermons became so popular they were reprinted in the newspapers. He writes in his autobiography, "When, for the first time, I received the gospel to my soul's salvation, I thought that I had never really heard it before, and I began to think that the preachers to whom I had listened had not truly preached it. But, on looking back, I am inclined to believe that I had heard the gospel fully preached many hundreds of times before," but this time "the power of the Holy Spirit was present to open my ear, and to guide the message to my heart." Previously, "the light was shining all the while, but there was no power to receive it; the eyeball of the soul was not sensitive to the Divine beams."[33]

Eminent twentieth-century Oxford/Cambridge don and Christian apologist C.S. Lewis entitled his autobiography *Surprised by Joy*: "But who can duly adore that Love which will open the high gates to a prodigal who is brought in kicking, struggling, resentful and darting his eyes in every direction for a chance to escape?" Lewis concludes, "the hardness of God is kinder than the softness of men, and his compulsion is our liberation."[34] A lion signals submission by crouching, resting its chin on the ground,[35] so we, too, must kneel at the judgment seat of Christ (Rom. 14:10–11). When Jonah was called to preach repentance in Nineveh, he, instead, took a ship going in the opposite direction. Soon he found himself in the belly of large fish. Upon being spit out, he agreed reluctantly to complete his

---

32. Chesterton, *Penguin Complete Father Brown*, 50.

33. Spurgeon, *C.H. Spurgeon's Autobiography*, Vol. 1, 102–3. Cf. Kerr, *Conversions*, 129–32.

34. Lewis, *Surprised by Joy*, 182–83.

35. Schaller, *Golden Shadows, Flying Hooves*, 127.

INTRODUCTION

assigned task. We may flee from God "down the nights and down the days," "down the arches of the years," "down the labyrinthine ways" of our own minds, "in the midst of tears" and "under running laughter," avows Francis Thompson in his famous poem, but the Hound of Heaven is not easily deterred.[36] God, like a stalking lion, doesn't give up the hunt easily. The king of beasts creeps "from bush to bush, halting whenever the quarry moves, then advancing again with such smoothness," observes naturalist George Schaller, "that one is barely conscious of movement."[37] That great twentieth-century French diplomat and playwright Paul Claudel once described his conversion this way, "I was like a man whose skin has been torn off with a single movement."[38] Maybe he did encounter a lion?

Nineteenth-century Catholic saint Therese of Lisieux relates how God spoke to her: "One Sunday when I was looking at a picture of our Lord on the cross, I saw the blood coming from one of his hands, and I felt terribly sad to think that it was falling to earth and that no one was rushing forward to catch it. I determined to stay continually at the foot of the Cross and receive it. I knew that I should then have to spread it among other souls."[39] She went on to conduct a ministry of intercessory prayer for even the greatest of sinners, for which she became legendary. God, it appears, does prefer to stay behind the scenes, lurking in the shadows. Paul urged the Philippians to "work out your salvation with fear and trembling;" while reminding them that it was God "at work in you, enabling you both to will and to work for his good pleasure" (Phil. 2:12–13). We often catch sight of what God is doing only years afterward, when a pattern begins to emerge from what previously had seemed a bewildering puzzle.

Finally, the lion is wild, untamed, unpredictable. "It is not the part of a true culture," warned Thoreau, "to tame tigers, any more than it is to make sheep ferocious."[40] An aggressive lion obliquely lowers its neck, stares straight ahead at its opponent with ears erect, then opens its mouth and snarls.[41] In the ancient world capturing lions was difficult; according to the naturalist Pliny the Elder, the most common method used for trapping them

---

36. Aldington, "The Hound of Heaven," *Viking Book of Poetry of the English-Speaking World, Vol. Two*, 1082–86.

37. Schaller, *Golden Shadows, Flying Hooves*, 152.

38. Mandeleker and Powers, *Pilgrim Souls*, 455.

39. St. Therese of Lisieux, *Autobiography*, 63.

40. Thoreau, *Excursions*, 212.

41. Schaller, *Golden Shadows, Flying Hooves*, 71.

INTRODUCTION

was covered pits.⁴² He reports that Hanno the Carthaginian was the first man who dared to handle a lion and to publicly display it tamed.⁴³ How many of you have ever been to the circus? There are so many daredevils—fire-eaters, tightrope walkers, a man who is shot out of a cannon—but the most riveting act of all, I find, is the lion-tamer. As whips snap, those roaring beasts will stand on their hind legs and jump through flaming hoops; but most scary of all, is when the tamer puts his head deep into the beast's jaws.

God can't be neatly pigeonholed or put inside a theological straitjacket, since he is the sovereign, sole ruler of the universe. He is sui generis, unique, in a category all by himself. His ways are altogether different from ours (Isa. 55:8). When Yahweh appeared on Mount Sinai to the people of Israel and handed the Ten Commandments to Moses, the people shrank back, stood afar off (Exod. 19–20). The scene is described in the Book of Hebrews (12:18–21): "You have not come to something that can be touched, a blazing fire, and darkness, and gloom, and a tempest, and the sound of a trumpet, and a voice whose words made the hearers beg that not another word be spoken to them. (For they could not endure the order that was given, 'If even an animal touches the mountain, it shall be stoned to death.' Indeed, so terrifying was the sight, that Moses said, 'I tremble with fear.')"

English mystery writer Dorothy Sayers once complained, "The people who hanged Christ never, to do them justice, accused him of being a bore—on the contrary, they thought him too dynamic to be safe. It has been left for later generations to muffle up that shattering personality and surround him with an atmosphere of tedium. We have very efficiently pared the claws of the Lion of Judah, certified him 'meek and mild,' and recommended him as a fitting household pet for pale curates and pious old ladies."⁴⁴

Let me share excerpts from two powerful, but contrasting, poems by mystic William Blake to illuminate this imagery of the lion-lamb.

> "Tyger! Tyger! burning bright
> In the forests of the night,
> What immortal hand or eye
> Could frame thy fearful symmetry? . . .

---

42. Pliny the Elder, *Natural History*, 115.
43. Pliny the Elder, *Natural History*, 116.
44. Sayers, *Letters to a Diminished Church*, 4.

> And what shoulder, & what art,
> Could twist the sinews of thy heart?
> And when thy heart began to beat,
> What dread hand? & what dread feet?"[45]
>
> Now here's the second:
> "Little Lamb, who made thee?
> Does thou know who made thee?
> Gave thee life, & bid thee feed
> By the stream & o'er the mead;
> Gave thee clothing of delight,
> Softest clothing, wooly, bright;
> Gave thee such a tender voice,
> Making all the vales rejoice?"[46]

A lion's paw may be velvet in friendship, but is frightful in battle.[47]

A moving modern example of leonine imagery is C.S. Lewis's *The Lion, the Witch, and the Wardrobe*. All of Narnia has been turned into winter due to the evil white witch. Animals have been frozen like statues. But Aslan, the rightful king, who is a lion, is now on the prowl, slowly unraveling the witch's spell through his human intermediaries Peter, Susan, Edmund, and Lucy, aided by all manner of beasts and mythological creatures. Aslan lets himself be subdued, tied down, and slain by the white witch. But she is unaware of the "deeper magic" of the universe; for "when a willing victim who had committed no treachery was killed in the traitor's stead, . . . Death itself would start working backwards."[48] Lo, Aslan is alive once more. This is an extraordinary picture of Jesus's own sacrifice on the cross for our sins and his ultimate triumph over death and the devil.

Let me relate a few more stories about lions from the medieval bestiaries; these are more allegorical, harder for those of us raised on realism to swallow. Lions, it is said, use their tails to hide their tracks, so the hunter is unable to follow them; just so did the Son hide his divinity from Satan in his human nature. Or, it was said, that a lion sleeps with eyes wide open, just so Christ went into the sleep of death on the cross, but his divine nature remained wide awake. And even more farfetched, lion cubs were believed

---

45. Frye, "The Tyger," *Selected Poetry and Prose of William Blake*, 43.
46. Frye, "The Lamb," *Selected Poetry and Prose of William Blake*, 24.
47. Ford, *Companion to Narnia*, 18.
48. Lewis, *Lion, Witch, and Wardrobe*, 133.

INTRODUCTION

to be born dead and then brought to life on the third day when their father breathed on them, just as the Father raised the Son to life on the third day.[49]

These are but a few of my observations of Christ as lion. The next time you go to a wildlife park or zoo, take a few minutes to contemplate that king of beasts. Consider: in what ways does he remind you of our Lord and Savior? Or choose some altogether different creature. The Book of Proverbs mentions lessons learned from hard-working ants, lizards who live in king's palaces, and the way roosters conduct themselves.[50] As Job famously remarked, "But, ask the animals and they will teach you." God's majesty and power have been made manifest in creation, if we had but eyes to see.

Prayer: All of nature continuously sings of you. Let us, like that fictional character in children's literature, Doctor Doolittle, learn to speak the language of animals,[51] so we can better discern what messages you are trying to convey. For we live in a sacramental universe, where each and every object we encounter, can, in the twinkling of an eye, as Ephrem the Syrian declares, become an emblem of your presence.[52] Amen.

---

49. White, *Book of Beasts*, 7–9. Cf. Biedermann, *Dictionary of Symbolism*, 209–10.
50. Prov. 30: 24–31. Cf. McDermott, *Everyday Glory*, 121.
51. Lofting, *Story of Doctor Dolittle*.
52. McVey, "Hymns on Virginity 20:12," *Ephrem the Syrian: Hymns*, 348–49.

The Spring Rain

The spring rain comes like the Alleluia of 1233
    or Edwards's Great Awakening—
in Amens and shouts of jubilation,
    Maranatha, tongues of diverse kinds.

It sinks like Bushnell's turtle,
    refurbishes Heaven's floor in green,
montage rhapsodies, crocus blues,
    hurdy-gurdy gossamer, yellow signatures.

Radial, bilateral, striped-arrayed,
    as spectacular as the Merry Monarch, Charles II,
poppies, dandelions, crab apple reds,
    Samson carries off the Philistine gates or asks his groomsmen riddles.

Molten rivers swollen up like Swiss Calvinist banks,
    multi-colored mists—here even God forgives a fool—
like St. Andrew's saltire binding the upper and lower spheres,
    diffraction grating prisms, God's Noahic troth.

Our mother earth soaks up all she can,
    then excretes the remainder to step brother Oceanus,
"Why do puddles pull at a little girl's boots?"
    the fibs of children like the lies the Cretans told.

There are five unlucky Mayan calendar days,
    Johnstown was swept downstream one May noon,
the greatest good is kind Fortuna,
    the second, foresight and preparation.

Sleep Comes Gently

Sleep comes gently to the country villa,
bluebells tinkling in the midsummer's breeze,
the praying mantis intoning vespers,
parachutes hang-glide from old cattails,
lady's slippers delicately prepare for bed.

No fairies' ballet on the tulip petals,
nor overactive chlorophyll troping for light,
only the nibble, nibble of Sir Aphid
voraciously ferreting his chemical tomb,
while a pale orb blinks an SOS
his genes seem unable to read,
a mottled Guernsey moos across the road,
two or three blossoms enter into Nirvana,
time lingers, yet goads by day,
and God winks at a post-lapsarian good.

A sans serif phlox twitches in the wind,
a baby's breath but twelve picas high,
a lonely daffodil among a cluster of pansies,
Bodoni bold lilacs commemorate the first fruits of those who sleep,
Indian paintbrushes shellack the peonies,
scarecrows defend from airborne assault,
come you strafing blackbirds, unfurl those beaks,
straw men will curtail your run.

A plaited morning glory chokes its mate,
a deep-throated sapsucker slurps its evening juice,
a pistil and stamen perform unspeakable acts,
a woodthrush lubricating his scales
to lead a feathered cacophony,
wild mustard and sourdock siphon off nutrients,
a cannibal plant munches on its prey,
Little Miss Spider crochets a mock-hammock
like an elderly church lady ensnaring her neighbor.

A bladderwort relieves itself on a nearby hen-and-chickens,
a painted lady flaps among the blazing stars
lowering her trumpet for nectar,
ladybugs cavort before their beaus,
creepy caterpillar tests out his latest springboard,
milkweeds spill over into the buttercups,
bastard toadflax gives illegitimate birth,
jack-in-the-pulpit putting away his Scriptures.

Where do the psyches of flora go
when wicked hands rip out the roots
or autumn knells a frosty execution,
does the earth suspend operation to replenish spring?
if this world were all, for the humanist
and not-so-humanist, I'd cry myself to sleep,
life's too delicate, too innocent, too gay,
to be snuffed out so soon.

Late Winter's Thaw

Mater Dolorosa,
pull down that crescent moon,
beautiful Persephone,
release your pomegranate red,
a virgin girdle's about to be loosened
—it's late winter's thaw!

When icy regret bends down your birches
and forlorn frost candies the meadows,
it's time for a ground hog supper
to break the north wind's subzero string.

In the vernal of our intentions,
a crocus cleft an elm,
the hoot owl screeched,
a raccoon is now displaced.

Blustery auburn superseded by black and olive,
muddied barnyards and snow in free-form shapes,
cooped-up children prance in red and yellow,
the water cycle more or less rejuvenated.

The north wind's back is karate cut,
the buds begin to pop,
matted clover as erect as little toy soldiers,
spores and sperms tossed in playful love,
the sluggish earth swings into awkward motion,
what of kites and their springy tails?

Stranger in an upheaved land,
newborn tremors, months of stale debris,
the old guard viraled off
to make room for minute change,
no Engels storming the Bastille,
but Brahman googol cycles.

Attis unmanned by Cybele,
Tammuz and grieving Ishtar,
this, the first foreshadowing,
winter's pain will be destroyed.

The Rainy Season

We're waiting for drops of rain,
but all that come are patches of mist, leftover dew,
intermittent threats of drizzle;
waterboy clouds scud by,
but no bucket leaks or even spills over.

World-weary trees put forth courageous buds,
nevertheless, are not about to blossom,
when the earth is clod-fisted tight,
the grass is thin, emaciated,
the shrubs, twisted exoskeletons.

Under the drab canopy cocoons are zippered shut,
drowsy seeds too chilled to pollinate,
all buzzing/stinging life lies dormant,
only rapacious weeds are anxious
to diffuse their promiscuous genes over any unclaimed site.

Meanwhile the earth mother scours the ethereal blue
for any who will soften her staid resolve with liquid kisses
to fatten her up with luxuriant child,
thus do perennials expose their intimate, most enticing parts,
excited damsels deign to mate in mid-air.

Still, nothing of consequence is going to happen until it pours,
miserly clouds release their hoarded guilders,
learn to be less puffy, independent, and more somber-serious,
in the new world the sterile aren't about to undergo regeneration
until the heavens split apart in torrents, cascades.

Fog

The marshmallow veil is densest in the bottoms,
there the elm and the maple are ethereal,
chlorophyll evaporates before the onslaught of inversion.

The fence posts play ring around the meadow,
the Holsteins seem a little hoarse,
the ivy and the clinging vine do embrace with soggy fingers,
might the aphids, too, put on their galoshes?

In the mountains the fog lifts up her petticoats,
a thrust fault encircled by gray underpants,
mesmerizing vista—you'd half expect Paul Bunyan and Babe the blue
to push up through the valley.

Cotton puffs, streaks of 75 percent reflection,
colors range from emerald green to opaque purple,
the air perspires, sweats up the grass,
till a 93-million-mile towel wipes it away.

The mammals have a sniffing apparatus,
the birds rely on magnetic compasses,
the plants pretend the sun has forfeited a circuit,
and man white-stares so pathetically.

Demystify the road to Qum,
penetrate the clouds of melancholy,
tear the fabric of agonizing tertiary,
the poppies still to heaven bent.

Hand-in-hand we groped for *Bedeutung*
in trackless byways, hit-or-miss alleys
populated by fleeing pigeons.

The wrath to burn off the layers of servile diffidence
congeals into pellets,
the minute it encounters hothouse imprecations.

No, I can't even locate my gyroscope
while balancing in a fog bank—
scaly wisps too delicate.

To a Waterfall

Liquid rainbow, unalloyed spritzer, torrent from another realm
leaping from ledge to ledge in a mad dash for repose,
scooping out craters, pelting limestone boulders,
swirling in funnel-shaped pools.

churning and tumbling and rinsing pollutants,
moistening the brush and any bystander,
gravity flow dispenser, conduit for spawning,
zebra light, checkerboard reflections, Tintoretto.

angry young cliffs or acute slaloms,
five-foot midgets you can build in your own backyard,
two hundred-meter spectacles worth a whole day's hike,
fog-enshrouded fairy tales, steady-state power stations.

turbulent spring or autumn trickle,
lush summer cascade or winter freeze-over,
bobbing willow branches, idyllic setting,
a faithful reproduction of Turner or Shingei.

roaring out politics and domestic squabbles,
atomizing anger, dissipating the dry light of reason
into foaming compassion, entrapping a chance reverie,
what a fine place to linger—*Dei gratia*!

Calling Upon the Wind

If we call upon the wind,
she can whistle a playful breeze
or blow up a relentless storm.

The Interminable Tedium of the High Plains

Imperceptible as the onset of a precision ruler
is the interminable tedium of the high plains,
deficient of all undulation, either intrusive or eroded,
there's progress to be sure, caesura, often,
but no gala Wagnerian movements,
just the simple metronome of synchronized grasses,
what kayak or schooner wouldn't founder
on this auburn permafrost,
what crew not succumb to mirages, vertigo
on the meandering shoals of these sienna waves?

One yearns for a tubular blast of basalt,
a hillside of metamorphic erratics,
limestone honeycombed with pink and flowing lava,
for this glacial terrain has been shaped by geometric cookie-cutters,
wrinkles stretched thin or pulverized
as a bricklayer's low-slung horizontal frame
imbued with pizzicato pastels,
such a crystallized sea is bald as a wig-maker's pate,
here the unfocused eye blunders across trackless wastes of savanna
devoid of Chimney Rock signposts.

The Desert as City

Organ pipe skyscrapers,
baked clay condominiums,
tumbleweed lanes,
the wandering dunes of time.

King Coyote and his crooners,
a sun-blanched arroyo,
24-hour blooms of prestige,
a Christmas cactus wearing a cherry yarmulke.

A saguaro cathedral,
a scorpion in pinstripes,
the feast of St. Helios,
parched delirium tremens.

Prickly pear housewives,
sidewinder lawyers,
bureaucratic prairie dogs,
bosses like the Great Horned Toad.

Shut up pores (evaporation rate 0),
the broken shards of my affection,
you're so despondent,
a thunderhead would pass you by.

Point a magnifying glass
at your (ouch!) needles,
and like the Syracuse mathematician
sink a battalion of mirages.

The Shore

On the splintered boardwalk
fake blue is pasted on green crystal,
barnacles syphon off the dock,
Ocean Grove is as serene as the first Sabbath,
gulls divebomb the fishermen,
the shoreline ripples over Billy's and Susie's toes,
the sand mudpacks your canvas shoes,
pipers flee before each fugal wave,
a toy lighthouse blinks at the surfer bums,
a child-sculptured castle encircled by a flooding moat,
water vapor fauna, a skiff
as wobbly as the *Titanic*,
salt-water jam, soda pop brine,
a picaresque setting for a *bildungsroman*,
clam spelunkers, treasure chest hounds,
flying tarpon, a baby with a sombrero,
a one hundred million-year-old surf
where two hundred thousand-year-old manikins play.

At the Beach

A crab's claw, shipwrecked jellyfish,
the valve of a clam wrenched open,
bits of nautilus, a lobster's exoskeleton,
a dead gull feet up, eyes gone,
beside a seahorse fallen from a boardwalk carousel.

Breakers

The breakers crash into the ocean floor
with the regularity of a pileated lunatic
beating his head against the hollow asylum wall.

Island Prisons

      Island prisons,
where marooned species proliferate,
their struggle for daily existence
has a coral, unending sameness,
like a medieval castle surrounded by
no-intruder walls and steep moats,
where xenophobic monks are locked into
Geʾez rites and read from Old Syriac Bibles,
crannies no fertilizing pilgrim has yet penetrated.

      Wingless: no predators,
undisturbed, mammoth, gluttonous tortoises,
still, migrating birds land and take off
from Patmos, Alcatraz, *Ile du Diable*,
isolation breeds Golding-like moans,
unheeded screeches for Pitcairn help,
history is washed up in seaworthy bottles,
mad, incoherent, blood-drenched survivors
nearly drowned at Atlantis or Krakatoa's obliteration.

      Conjecture replaces irrefutable fact
in Herodotus and Mandeville's travels,
striped papaya, palm seeds the size of a coconut,
communally-shared pearls, open,
unprivate huts, naked, excitable breasts,
the old world's taboos have been dropped
on the periphery of this atoll Arcadia,
where rainbow-prismed lizards crouch
and strike with dart-like venomous tongues.

In the Turquoise Deserts of the Sea

In the turquoise deserts of the sea
there are no shimmering plankton
or Sargasso oases of green,
it's a mineral-less wasteland,
waves like worms aerate the soil,
spores seldom send up playful shoots,
quanta packets of energy pour down,
yet few are the photosynthesis factories in active operation.

I saw mirages, silica dunes,
sailors, sun-parched, hauling crates of grain,
as though journeying through a nutrient-dead land,
generally it's best to carry one's own canteen,
for salt is liquid death,
fathoms below, creepy phosphorescent shapes
emerge beyond where pearl divers reach.

Above is the uninhabited, aborted Atlantis
(unstable, turbulent clime where few niches can survive),
below this Arctic surface lies a surreal Eden reversing the ecology
    of the land—
cold is harsh, unpredictable, and capable of mass extinction,
while tropical is flourishing, primeval, species-rich—
so the ocean floor, although frigid, is downright Amazonian,
ships cross over the bleak, warm, barren tundra.

Carefree

I'm blowing dandelions
in carefree May,
puffing on calumets
beyond the pillars of Hercules,
sipping my red Bordeaux
in the cave of the nymphs.

Upon Finding a Flower Blooming

Upon finding a flower blooming
that hadn't been open the day before,
I marveled at its sheer, radiating contours,
probed deep inside its cool, glistening petals,
dusted my palm by shaking out gold specks.

How can such unadorned splendor appear without hoopla,
the ordinary become infused with spiritual tones?
Germination seems slow and wasteful as seeds fall indiscriminately
    among thorns,
yet one day I came across such exquisite streaks of glory,
I thought I had been walking in the garden of gods.

The Lilies

The lilies have their treasures
in their throats,
not black-tumbler, casement-shut,
bolted, iron-grille,
electronic surveillance,
alarm bell, rifle/bayonet defended
steel vaults.

Water-Lily Beauty

The water lilies in their sparkling beds
whirlpool us much like beauty's forbidden gaze,
poisonous as the dart frog's grainy glands,
we long to strip and swim and bathe.

Ulysses twined against that reverberating mast,
lest the three Graces' garlands soak him in flowers;
from Delilah's entangled loops,
abracadabra! into Cleopatra's outstretched form.

Apollo hunted Daphne
until her love was dry as cork,
Herod lost his head
over Salome's unseemly spinning.

Misty Rhine castles, bullroarer vibrations,
water-blossom Antilles,
the formaldehyde beauty of death juxtaposed,
when alluring sirens call, our footing breaks loose.

Tumbling Nests

Nests come tumbling down
like poorly-thatched huts quavering on proverbial sand,
slipshod, makeshift, incomplete,
haphazard, trendy, tilting,
constructed with little regard for eventualities,
later on one could make amends,
in the meantime let's push on,
though the clay's improperly drained,
the pegs poorly pounded, the walls all askew,
untested saplings serve as joists or beams,
no litany of sacrifices and intercessions could ever compensate
for a wobbly superstructure or a feeble frame.

Without so much as a thunderclap, disaster struck,
what's flimsy couldn't survive,
passersby nod as though prescient of impending fiasco—
stress and tension irregularities accumulate,
shoddy innards are incrementally eaten away,
devil-may-care fatalism leads to collapse.

Despite blueprints and schematics from master designers,
I believe nests will continue to freefall,
as they have neither bounce-back nets nor rubber, resilient eggs,
even on a warm, uneventful July forenoon,
the skies may be rent with churning straw and mud.

Broadcast, Don't Drill

The summer emerald is daubed with russet and olive,
the tomatoes, pumpkins, melons take on a ribald hue,
the diligent hoeing, weeding, and cutting back
reap golden dividends and interest manifold.

So the patient turtle collects and the crazed hare
dashes from lottery to lottery, expecting instant millions,
I, too, cultivate and mulch my Occidental/Oriental fields,
pulling up here a flower, there a bulbous fruit.

The cooling breeze, the fast-sinking yellow ball
enunciate the guillotine and the lopping off
of this year's assortment of rebels and priests,
the faithful scythe knows not caste distinctions.

I weep a little for friends I've known,
more decadent, I choose younger, finer playmates,
the carefree, wanton days of June
turn into September's stratagems and fears.

The harvest for which I labored
now seems egocentric and tainted,
the overripe, drooping branches
paralyze my knees.

The grains filling up bucket after bucket
are like pirate doubloons
plucked from a sunken galleon.

I should have broadcast,
not planted row after row
of identical, immune-deficient hybrids,
or matured them
at two or three dates.

Now this whopping harvest
is ugly, blighted,
fodder fit only for burrowing worms.

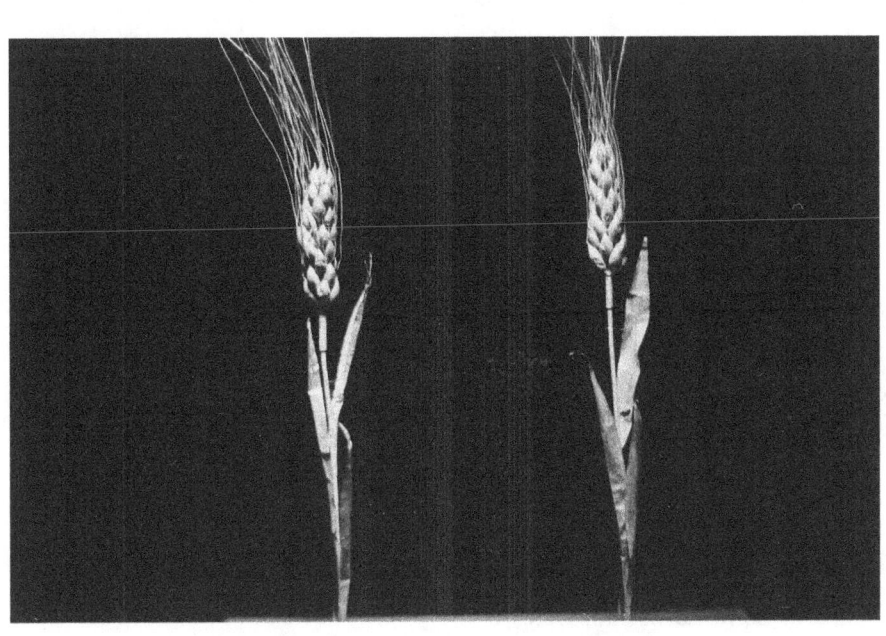

Bumper Ennui

In the snow apple orchard I hear the wiggly worm
—half-digested greens, stomach cramps—
fruit flies, dehydrated sap, life wrinkled up
into robust red and sassafras maize,
the slopes of Uttarakuru crushed by
ripe purple plums, muskmelons split
open in Nature's exuberance.

I crouch to avoid a bough
requiring a cesarean section,
the podded soybeans and dented ears
of Dekalb-241; the knell of the harvest
decapitates the rye; from the Panhandle
to Saskatchewan seasonal migrants
make a swath of wheat and sorghum mounds.

I circumcise a hop for Bacchus,
light up some kernels for Ceres,
too many sprouts, too many buds,
too many acres of gold, broken-down combines,
dog-tired apple-pickers, bumper ennui,
a cornucopia albatross that deflates
the rural economy,

a duty-free tithe of minuscule proportions,
cider till it bursts your gullet,
black-sodded nutritional excess,
grace that lends itself to vomit,
the summer ends not with a thud
but with a wallop, an encore dénouement,
a blasé Puritan Thanksgiving.

The Dangling Tomatoes

The dangling tomatoes
on their spindly vines,
mottled green and yellow,
bursting red, smooth
as nectarines, pucker up,
slippery seeds
profuse as a watermelon's.

You bite and squish
the sourest fruit
that ever carmine stained
vermilion tongue.

Pumpkins and Gourds

The orange, rotund Emperor of the Fall
amid his yellow, dimpled guards.

Ungovernable Fingers

Forcing the fruit from the vine
with impatient, ungovernable fingers.

The Corn Palace

Walls decorated with strawberry/Indian corn,
a palace of hard-shell maize,
here the Midwest's munificence
is forced into Moorish amber and vermilion,
Iroquois wampum into popping mural beads.

I bless the sky for filling the ear with lactose nourishment,
honor the tassel for wind-blown zygote displays,
do homage to the lean, vigorous "mammary" stalks
that bear their young to full silk maturity.

The split cotyledon, that Rodin embryo of regeneration,
sprouts from the food of its dead parents:
cornbread, cornmeal, corn tortillas,
corn nuts, corn chowder, caramel-flavored balls.

I've tasted enough of these starchy delicacies
to know that from organic, vitamin-rich glacial/alluvial sod
carbohydrates can please the most discriminating, raspish ungulate tongue.

That's why the squirrels and blue jays munch on such biodegradable
     sculpture
before touching the Old World's linseed oils,
consecrating these pebbled frescoes, cracking open
their molded pretensions to immortality.

These Damnable Flies

These damnable flies
ogling your stale crumbs,
circle, land, and refuel
like squadrons of Luftwaffe bombardiers,
rubber suction-cup your kitchen sink,
anxious to hatch their mucous larvae
in the aorta of your oven-baked pie.

Their auditory turbulence would disturb
a Diogenes or Stylites,
their diversionary tactics
are worth a reference or two in von Clausewitz,
their Medusa heads are more sickening than Dorian Gray's
decadence compounded by disease and brutality,
hysteria, *chorea lascivia* on wings.

Shoo them away
and they'll surge through some blasted hole in the screen,
swat 'em and they'll dancing-escape,
more wily than the grouper's color schematics,
catch 'em on sticky paper,
the sidewalk grows refuse-cluttered by squalid black shapes,
even the asthmatic's glass walls are specked with their telltale droppings.

In nightmares I'm pinioned beneath huge, bristling claws,
feelers, like Caligari's somnambulist, stroke my paralyzed sides,
wings flutter and beat till I disgorge my innermost secrets
when threatened by compound eyes and proboscis,
mouthparts which would sever my torso,
I cried from the belly of this Poe monstrosity,
Lord, if you will, deliver me from the scourge of super 8mm horror.

The Prey

Often have I been torn apart by maddened beasts,
maimed by tusks, felt the thrust of swordfish,
known the rasping paw to pry open my hardened shell,
too, I've been fired at, skinned, and hung above the mantel,
sewn into a mottled shawl, fashionable hat, or scale purse,
felt the arrow's intruding head,
beheld colored illusions from the poisoned dart,
cringed at the cudgel's lethal blow.

Too, I've been caught in saw-toothed traps, bit into metal hooks,
been drawn by a pseudo-mating call,
flown up and become entangled in a mist net,
been pecked at by mangy buzzards,
drowned and left to rot in the stinking crocodile's lair,
I've felt the pincers of jagged mandibles,
been stretched out, bound to bamboo poles, and roasted by hungry natives,
strangled headlong by a wily, reticulated python,
or stung, paralyzed and stored as lunch for voracious larva.

Which edible fate would you choose?

For Fluffy

Tickle a cat
and he'll drop a mouse,
rub your whiskers against his chin,
bird feathers might pop out,
sniff at those saber paws,
watch the knives unsheathe.

Wind that stand-up tail,
he'll spin and bite and yowl,
smooth out that lionesque mane, remove some burr,
he'll knead like a playful doll,
lick him to insure a friend,
he'll oval nest upon your lap
or hang from your shoulders ready to pounce.

Cradle him like baby Bunting
and he'll shiver and purr and purr,
basking in your peculiar scent,
even misanthropes are quite overcome.

The Animal Game

Howl like a hyena,
swing like a baboon,
back float like the sea otter—
front paws on your chest,
scoop up salmon
like the grizzly,
spit and squeal like the mink,
molt seasonally like the snowshoe rabbit,
bound on your hind legs
like a kangaroo rat,
thump your tail like a beaver,
burrow like a shrew mole,
slither like a sidewinder,
grab your young by the scruff of their neck
like a Serengeti leopard,
swell up like the puffer,
sniff as a kiwi
with the tip of your beak,
like the fruit bat
hang upside-down from the rafters,
nap as a toucan:
chin on your back,
stare goofy-eyed at each other
like passionate lovebirds,
take off and land
as a helicopter mallard,
hover iridescently like a hummer,

sink like the grebe submarine,
dive with the frigate,
waddle like a pintail,
soar silver-winged like an albatross,
swivel your eyes independently
much as a chameleon,
bray like a mule,
walk on the water
like a tiptoeing basilisk,
flap your elephant ears as Dumbo,
then signal your mate
just like the fiddler crab.

Breakthrough

Fertilize,
then incubate,
till the chick pecks through
its claustrophobic Edwardian shell.

Hope

Hope perches in the highest rafters,
I've seen it crash through cupola and dome,
molt wings on the pinnacle of steeples,
telegraph its reverberations down.

Like the Grecian Titans, it flattens heaven's door,
Icarus comet-scorches, eager to rout Brother Sol,
Hope warbles through an eclipse,
cranes its beak skyward, regardless of the wind.

"Grumble—grumble" croaks the bullfrog,
"Hiss—hiss" choruses the snake,
"Sputter—sputter" careens the damselfly,
"My tonic and gin?" noisy, belligerent Man.

Above a bed of worms Hope blue jay teases,
carps about our hunch-shouldered walk,
a few ascetic butterflies shimmering take off,
but the majority of pupae just shrivel up and drop.

Congratulatory Feedback

The dog who breaks open a bone
believes he sucks the marrow of a mastodon.

Noah and the Ark

Animals scurry pell-mell
to that fabled ark
to hide themselves
in the cleft of his palm,
against torrential downpours,
cataclysms, record-breaking tides,
they seek safety in wooden promises,
"a three-tiered Renaissance hotel,"
371 thankful days of "hibernation,"
buffeted by hunger, persecution,
cackling scoffers and realists,
their anchor holds secure
within the gopherwood and pitch.

When faith seems at ebb,
there appears a red and violet arc,
a faint, secondary bow, colors reversed,
once God dismissed the primeval couple
from the Garden of Delights,
a second time he'll wash the chariots of
hard-hearted Pharaoh in rivers of blood,
but for now he sends *shalom* symbols—
olive leaves and doves—
honors the blood of mute, suffering animals,
docks his sea-weary band
of Bradford and pilgrims
to colonize a harsh, intemperate Canaan.

The evangelium they carry:
murder must be requited,
kosher food slit open before served,
vague, inscrutable glimmerings
of Messianic redemption.

An Imaginative Exercise for William James[1]

If I could sniff the colors of the wind,
taste the wave-harmonics of a full-throated nightingale,
listen in to the obsessive perfume of a raw, sensual caress.

These would be odd criss-crossings indeed,
as though some relay switch had been left open, the current rerouted past
   a circuit breaker;
it's nigh unto impossible to distinguish between competing senses.

A fuzzy peach puckers up my earlobes,
can you tune a purple banana or a black tangerine?
does a symphony stink like rafflesia,
suppose whole grains smacked of monochrome?

Let's try once more:
can you measure the intensity of a hue with a stethoscope?
wrap your fingers around an excited flat or sharp?
taste the vapors inside a photograph?

These are elementary feats, indeed, for the accomplished virtuoso,
who has no need for a grab bag of new technologies,
just synesthesia, a free-floating, crosshatched imagination.

---

1. Underhill, *Mysticism*, 7.

The Flood of Time

To hold back the flood of time
before it 'whelms us all,
I place my finger in its core,
where milliseconds beat and trickle
and rush to that fateful shore,
still the pendulum, still the isotope,
decaying half-life after half-life,
I feel its heart,
the effusive liquid throbs,
man puts out his stay.

Time is the river
where we wash our filthy hands,
pristine from its source; downstream:
pollution and sludge, in it we paddle
and float, though the current may be gentle
or wreak havoc at each bend,
I snatch at twigs, uprooted stumps,
while sucked toward its all-gorging mouth,
sediments accumulate, salt water seeps in,
eco-niches change, prestissimo I vanish.

A Utopian Solution

If we could seed and harvest oceans,
stack air plants in three-dimensional rows,
irrigate deserts with rain forest run-off,
periodic famines might yet be reversed.

The World's the Bride

The world's the bride I'll take,
sugarcoated, lime-green virgin stands,
lacey-white, smoking hot silkworm bodice,
forbidden beauty—Justinian penned in for my delight.

The fragrance of exotic Ceylon oils,
the nudesome glory of Niagara or Yellowstone,
far grander melodies I hear beyond our Milky Way,
yet divorce not I, your cordilleran contours, for that paler sight.

Some reckless lovers fashion mock-Edens in their brain,
forsake now, for eschatological pleasures hence,
yet banquet I and burst my passion's fill,
like the paraffin and cord in heated matrimony.

In the Valley of Jehoshaphat my bones will be as dry as yours,
strange joys I'll know—but they will take getting used to,
weaned from sorrow and Echo's moans,
I'll float like Saturn on an ocean of aphrodisiacs.

Watteau's flowers, birds, trellises, *ornaments decoratifs*
bind us with their pearly loins;
before the silver cord snapped,
the tomb of Pope Julius was Michelangelo's cross to bear.

Then let us, like children dear,
criss-cross maypole ribbons here,
like the scurrying ant and buzzing bee,
conjoin our interests in the realm of concrete forms.

Thoughts of Human Grandeur

I demolished thoughts of human grandeur
when I walked past El Capitan.

Creation Groans On

Creation groans on in anticipation
and shall I droop forlorn
as forget-me-nots at the end of the season?

Will tomorrow's hues be
more resplendent than yesterday's,
a heaven of gold untarnished by innuendo?

Is eros a foretaste of the new Jerusalem
or just some fleeting concession
that reminds us of our mortality?

Are words themselves a fractured medium
too subtle or too ambiguous
to carry a message from another realm?

Is mystic warmth far too subjective
to influence our peers,
my light—your hallucination?

To what shall we liken
the negative attributes of God,
does silence reverberate louder than sign language?

Is sublunary truth so slender,
skinny as your common pancake fish,
a crevice no van Leeuwenhoek has yet deciphered?

Or does the honeybee hum a secret tune
of joy and supernatural birth,
too pristine and simple for our egocentric ears?

Bless the Lord

All that yearn for gentler habitations
—Bless the Lord.
Bless him my sin-wracked,
volcanic, double-speak lips.

Air and mineral water, underground sinkholes,
undulating land masses
—Honor him with gifts appropriate to his name.

Birds that glide, spin and soar
with grace no zeppelin has challenged
—Bring him laud and dignity ethereal.

You beasts of the field and pouched mammals
    —Offer up your wool, your hide,
    may your fat form his tallow,
    your muscles nourish his nabob, man.

You fish of the sea with limpid color,
stern-eyed, cavorting among the kelp
in riotous, darting passions
—Rejoice in your Creator.

You plants striving for the sun,
> put out reproductive stamen,
> array the earth with Louvres,
> each hour a new and bolder masterpiece
—Give him his green luxuriant due.

The periodic chart cracks open, combining rare elements
> with those more rare,
overheated rocks belch forth their steaming lava,
while the pinpoints of the night reflect his fusion power.

Man, too, raises up his aggrieved, belligerent voice,
sets out his gifts in lacquered bronze,
pursues know-nothing, ill-considered, unmanifest destinies,
rains curses on all curbs of self-restraint
—Bless him, you *Dummkopf*.

Chewable Spirituality

Monks, pious as pretzels,
nuns, contemplative as romaine lettuce.

God Wants Only Lambs

God wants only lambs
—not pythons, alligators, or panthers—
desiring the tame, the docile, the unclawed.

Sheep grow frightened by a booming stranger,
run for cover at the whiff of a wolf or coyote,
will pasture defenseless in a field of carnivores.

When in danger they bleat unabashedly for their one True Shepherd,
will offer up their fleece for the greater flock,
lay down their own lives for a wounded comrade.

God longs for any who are unpretentious, companionable, vulnerable,
who'll lick the salt right off your toes,
he dwells in the holy of holies of their twice-born hearts.

A Morbid Autumn

In October the blood's spilt on the trees,
a hillside littered by a hundred miniature Calvaries,
the oak's heart is ripped apart
and flings its arterial flow
down mountain slopes and vacant stream beds,
every meadow is sprouting abscesses and hemorrhaging wounds,
the Rose of Sharon's pricked
in a crimson petal waterfall.

I see the Hanged Man's ankles and wrists
profuse as a martyr's fountain,
bucket upon bucket of vermilion
flutter down from that tree trunk sepulcher,
like some angry, suffering god twisted up
in sin-crackling knots and burls,
the wood resounds, the aspen quake,
the Pierced One returns after a two-thousand-year hiatus.

His skeleton is stripped bare
save for this tumbling, atoning red,
the children bathe themselves in the desiccated veins,
are made righteous by the sprinkling of lobes drained of chlorophyll.

Tumble-Down Crosses

In a cemetery of tumble-down crosses
a dwarf, lip-red rose is blooming,
below a turbulent thunderhead
tender shoots escape from incorruptible seed,
within a rectangle of decrepit fenceposts
larvae are discarding pupa gowns,
at the boundary between *bios* and *thanatos*
lines of demarcation blur,
amino acids return to the subsoil,
while the soul-supreme assumes a more liberated form,
just as the womb's bones are transfigured into the laughing child,
so earthly flesh is more fully constituted in spiritual terms,
take off your quivering shoes,
this is numinous ground.

Though rigid stones lean against the morning air,
megalith reminders of some ancient cataclysm,
whisperings, murmurings, green tufts of immortality
hint at, suggest, as if in gay anticipation,
that the universe's law is to revive again.

I'll Be Transformed

In an instant
I'll be transformed,
in the twinkling
of an eyelash
and a blare
from Gabriel's horn,
when the veil is punctured,
a new scenario is made known.

Before atoms
can disintegrate,
fire scour
our earthly mantle,
when Gog and Magog
head off for battle,
the Son of Perdition
be revealed,
our bleeding Conqueror
will appear.

If those days
had not been shortened,
all deluded flesh
would wreak violence—
graceless, idolmongers—
destructive impulses
unabated, in overdrive.

Ask the dumb animals;
listen to their tales:
there's the crocodile who weeps,
a tigress nursing
her glass reflection,
the cuttlefish gnawing
off his tentacles,
the obtuse, lecherous ass,
man, too, enwebbed
in his lucre.

Pure as an ermine
I must ascend,
like the hibernating bullfrog
or Antony of Padua's faithful mule
kneeling for communion,
I must bleat with the lambs,
soar as a falcon,
then, in the likeness of a dove,
perhaps I'll be changed.

Absolute Zero

All clocks pointing to one fateful hour,
tulips poised, ready to unfurl their petals,
when lost opportunity is forever preserved in crystal,
the signal stuck equally between the sender and the receiver—
    Absolute zero.

Water bearer's contents poured but won't come out,
being solidifies into inert spheres,
when praxis hardens into Enlightenment orthodoxy,
the spider, this once, too slow to claim its prey,
    Stroke or paralysis.

Behemoths basking in envelopes of ice,
cursing words break before they strike the ground,
when tenderness becomes caked with sloth,
the penis stalled in the wrong vagina—
    Brain death.

The black widow male refusing immolation,
the biennial tuber stored for naught,
when hope lies buried under a reverse fault,
the praying mantis unwilling to gesticulate before his god,
    Second coming.

Death like a Vine

Death like a vine
clambered up our wall
and entered through an open window,
there stretched out
his leathery fingers,
startled the whole house
with dirges, lamentation,
then silent as a lock picked,
the destroyer returned,
earth-to-earth, to his hairy roots,
mission accomplished.

Unbelief

Unbelief gathers momentum like gravity,
its mass is constant, avoirdupois strong,
its fall perpendicular, its thud autumn leaf soft.

Faith grunts toward its supersensual object
in threadbare, porcupine hairshirt,
the destination—Pisgah or Purgatory—gore.

The rind—lack of conviction—mouth-watering smooth,
scalpels are all but unnecessary,
the injections? Gerber's intravenous solution.

The diet of martyrs: sugar-coated enzyme gruel,
the acids eat out your wallpaper gullet
from pink to alkaline blue.

The Hidden Things of God

The heavens above the heavens serenade my heart,
where spiral gases tell of lovelorn, pregnant stars—
like the merits we accumulated as children
spattered from the meridian to the horizon.

Through my scope I see Taurus and Leo,
animals and gods from Homer to Ovid,
a hand sowing galaxies as farmers do fields,
some will flourish, some wilt, some be overwhelmed by invaders.

I am thunderstruck at the hidden things of God,
what cybernetic being requires an aqualung?
what manned sputnik e'er broke out the Milky Way?
we who invent a new widget presume like Augustus towards deity.

If we should hap upon some less reprehensible race,
well, the church bells would peal paeans to man,
or should some kindhearted ruler take us in tow,
perhaps we'd be in Egypt a mere three thousand years.

As infinite as life might have been,
cross two hawkweeds, you won't come up red,
Bruno knew of worlds heaped up on worlds,
but Clement VIII thought one sufficient unto death.

The distances, the colors, the igneous in its molten state,
the conjectures, the vistas—still the harsh underbelly of the universe
  is exposed—
sitting on three-dimensional coordinates,
I gawk like Adam and give Latin names.

Incalculable Things

Who can count all the pulverized granules of sand?
take a census of an ocean full of floating things?
measure the exact distance between two opposite spiraling galaxies?
roughly estimate the number of hominids since the beginning of creation?
the ratio of microbes to each terrestrial cubic centimeter?
determine the voltage of attraction between the doting sexes?
conjecture on the allotropes of some synthetic, undiscovered periodic
    element?

construct a mood scale registering a graduated spectrum of intensities?
delineate the line of demarcation between vegetable and mineral matter?
forecast the consequences of an all-out nuclear winter?
Aquinas-like catalogue the perverted projections of the numinous?
launch a flashing Kantian probe to dissect a neighbor's naked intentions?
formulate the factors that differentiate "civilization" from "barbarism"?
chart the increase in stars due to the additive power of each new lens?
irradiate the range of pulsating beams penetrating our atmosphere
    undetected by human eyes?

define the canons of aestheticism or, at least, rigorously outline the elements
    of play?
tunnel to the core of our igneous inferno to establish colonies regardless
    of climatic extremes?
spell out the connotations and denotations of each phalanx of Anglo-Saxon
    terms?
fashion a plastic representation of what goes on in a chimpanzee's head?

rescue all lost civilizations, well then, recover just the missing *adonics* of Sappho?

communicate as a native, incarnate in all known genera and species?

clone a robot that will correct its errant maker?

rearrange the chromosomes, so only upwardly-striving, euphonious genes will win?

distinguish the real cause from its parasitic host of antecedents?

enumerate the consequences of one casual, albeit deliberate, lie?

form a genealogical table of sin with complete cross-references and repeated offenses in bold?

Are you able, willing, and eager?

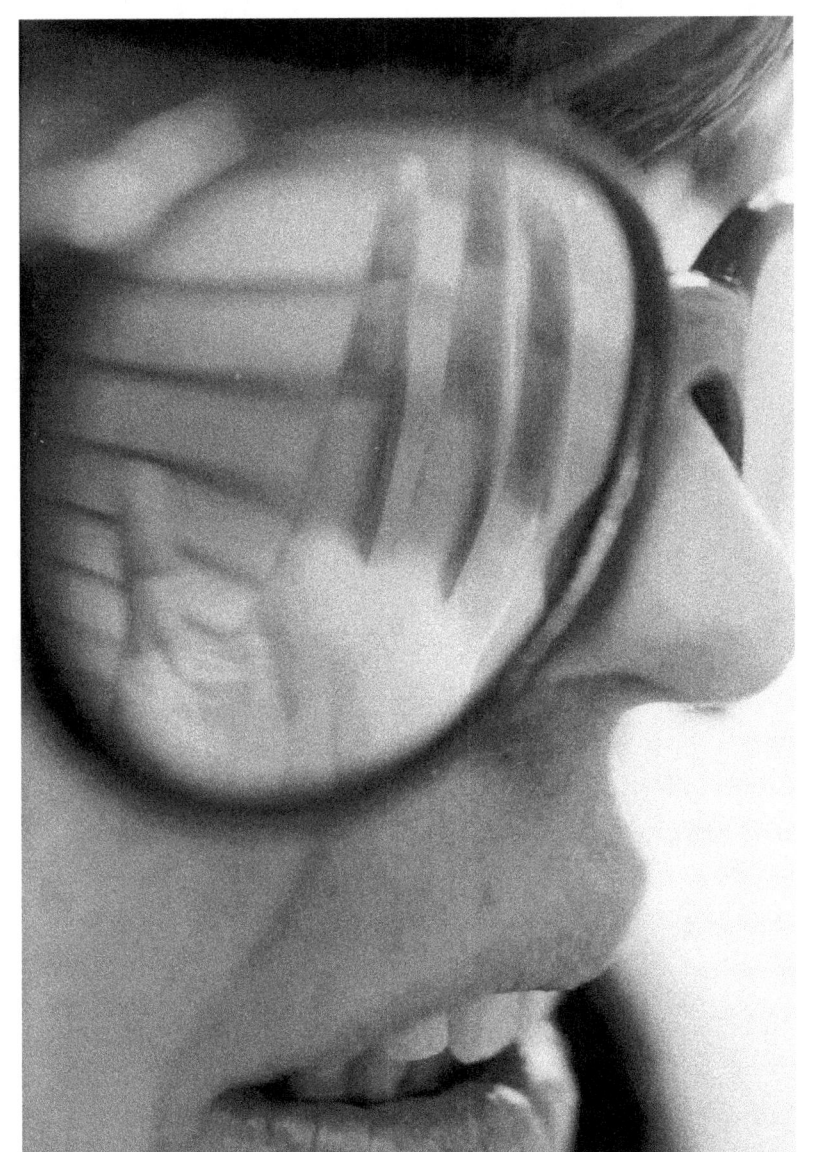

Maya

Maya, the eternal spider,
spins her illusory web.

Space . . .

Melt down the saints into hollowed nickel,
press your mucous lips against my withered folds,
sprinkle the dehydrated plasma over the sacrificial lamb,
suffuse the rotted cavity with liquid silver.

Space poured, squeezed, wrapped up with your lingerie,
buffeted, supercharged and blasted through the tuba's snout,
space drilled into a nozzle and aimed at an emerald bead,
cajoled to condense,
woofed and tweeted by a tuning fork,
sealed out of mama's jam.

Almost weightless, depending on the elevation,
knotted up inside a membrane, bubbling through the gills,
dwarfs growth when too congested,
expandable in the open air,
partitioned into cubicles, swirled up the nautilus,
cast and set on an assembly line.

Amorphous echo, absolute frequency,
stampeded into symmetry by a celestial gush
or an Einstein curvature, shoved into the void
along with Aristotle, entropy disturbed
to an infinitesimal degree by the primordial gong,
swelled and shrunk like an accordion,
a pneumatic thunderhead.

In the beginning was immaterial God,
the monotheistic constant, immanent and transcending,
whose center is everywhere and circumference is nowhere,
starts his deistic stopwatch, says Enlightenment orthodoxy, then croaks.
Exhale and inhale till the python wends you home.

The Shadow

The angle of declension cuts out a dark facsimile
as accurate as the fun-house looking glass,
ugly black or gray,
dripping features as definitive as the elastic android,
deprives plants of a percentage of their due,
like a glorified body which partitions molecules,
zero gravity, thickness minuscule,
extends in two directions like a washed-out negative.

A Punch and Judy free-for-all,
a labyrinthine diversion for Aristotle,
from satellite photos Interpol draws a rogues' gallery of silhouettes,
obtuse, impenetrable, tag-along as a cocker spaniel,
the whiter its environs, the more luxuriant it glows,
the bluntest member of your entourage,
can terrify the weaned babe or snatch the *élan vital* of an aborigine,
yet on a cloudy day be reluctant to come out and play.

If you chance upon this solemn fellow,
let him be the first to speak,
or if arrogance you esteem,
challenge the swaggerer and see who first cries, "Ouch,"
at noon he's more the midget, trounce him while you may
—he's all poor Plato's chained captives knew of true forms,
an illusion Macbeth mistook for disembodied being.

Hades and Sheol are cluttered with these emasculated things,
while in holy Jerusalem, the Lamb usurps their rights,
    witness a foretaste of that brightness,
      honey, now flick off the light.

Time, That Fleeting Deer

Time, that fleeting deer,
prancing through my meadow,
puffy tail and pointed ears,
no wolves to speed you up or slow you down.

Hold up, I say,
why not a little duet today?
I've half a mind to call your bluff
and see if you can show your stuff . . .

Kairos, now seize the bower
or find yourself locked in London tower,
Chronos hath a more steady gait,
with a little more practice he'll make do.

Oh, go on then you silly fawns,
prance and prance forever on,
but there'll come another day,
then I'll plead and perhaps you'll stay.

On Gathering Stars

Let us fill our pockets with flecks of light,
    while they frosty glisten
    in lackluster December.

Let us pull longest and hardest
    on those *in extremis* Paradise
    beyond the dipper and Arcturus.

Shall we grasp the molten with the cooled,
    the metamorphic and the sedimentary,
    till asters radiate and diffuse?

Yes, I say, let others sink their derricks,
    blast tunnels through mountain ore,
    as for me, I'll be gathering bouquets of pretty stars.

Signs of the Zodiac

Some nights I wander out among the stars,
shivery as Arcturus, steaming as Betelgeuse,
along that stretch of blazing white
I throw out a worm for Pisces,
blink red in Taurus's eyes,
lunge right through the heart and split up Siamese Gemini,
quaff down a serum from Aquarius's spout,
inquire directions of the Virgin to this galaxy's outer shell,
twirl Capricorn by his fish tail,
whip my ship past Leo's fierce whiskers
till Aries comes from his thicket,
test the gravitational attraction between planetary bodies
on Libra's delicate balance,
veer first to the right to evade Sagittarius,
then take a hard left against Scorpio's poisoned slingshot,
finally scuttle off after the ghost crab,
the stars are meant for those of bulbous, second sight,
yet how many of us have ventured out to their imagined shores?

Song of a Shaman

I sit, shaking a gourd rattle,
intoning an age-old tribal chant,
should I raise an eagle feather,
put a blue cactus over my left ear,
I can feel the power come down
for the night is robust with outsized visions.

First, Master Coyote chases Nimble Rabbit,
my brethren, have no fear of him,
Field Mouse gnaws on Desert Cricket,
we have become half-famished, half-surfeited,
Spotted Bird soars high above the glacial peaks,
the battle may yet turn and we rout our enemies,
the Moon is clotted with lime spume,
a third of the stars have hibernated,
turquoise toads swim in a lavender sea.

Great and High Spirit, everywhere impiety rages,
young people have departed from the ancient guideposts,
while feathered dancers swirl in a gruesome bloodletting,
stop their circular agony.
Give me, the hereditary shaman, the key to all disease,
for Brown Bear is ravaging upper forest,
Summer Stag appears with peeling antlers,
Yuma Warriors string together bow upon bow of poisoned arrows.

Oh, that the Old Ones would stop transmitting horrid pictures and sounds,
why should I be a conduit for their anger?
weak and emaciated after months of fasting—
friends carry me to the dying tent,
the smoke of my life nears the vent-hole,
should I recover, the spirits will demand harsher and harsher sacrifice,
is tomorrow a stubborn, indifferent gray?
is there no light on the morning rim?

How Do You Wake Up?

Some wake up with the sunlight glistening on their lips,
extend the previous evening's activities reinvigorated,
others, drab as night, eyes sunk in like a deep staring owl's,
dreams disoriented as the groggy earth's,
stare at pent-up menacing claws.

Some wake up bubbling, with effervescence on their brows,
bound off the high springboard, require no morning stimulant,
others must be coaxed, wheedled, all-screaming into the tepid water,
can't quite puncture the surface film, doubt all value of buoyancy,
madly paddle about a swirling vortex.

Some leap instinctual as gazelles,
pace themselves unhurried before a host of ferocious pursuers,
others flounder, run amuck, squarely hit a dead wall,
refuse to jump the high hedge, surrender in full regalia,
yelp, but find no responsive bystander.

Some are born self-possessed, spendthrifts on the morrow,
perceive far-off sequential implications, expectations increase exponentially,
others, at the base of citrus, pull down unripe fruit,
never experience Sun Dance visions or perform supersonic feats,
just don a shroud for premature burial.

Sunset

When the earth mother swallows her solar pill,
she burps up weakened light—magenta,
crimson, or coral—transposes her feverish hues
into an iridescent body of song,
like Theodoric's rainbow flask,
one prism boost-refracting another.

At sunset we age so beautifully,
gone is the arthritic stigma of flaunting mortality,
a beatitude of calm sets us on Mount Carmel's summit;
the fleshpots of Memphis, Sparta's patriot frenzy,
Jacob supplanting Esau's title deed—
flow gently into pumice holes.

Our Lady of the Stars mellows us along with sting rays,
scorpions and jellyfish, soothes "we who are not alone";[2]
should one planet fireball fizzle across the void,
another permutation might succeed,
and our puny hurrahs evaporate
when measured against the *tzimtzum* whole.

---

2. Sullivan, *We Are Not Alone*.

On the seventh day Yahweh slept,
who had hung the earth without a thread,
the waters of Meribah were stilled at Hezekiah's pool,
and all the choleric atoms stream toward entropy,
man toiled outside Eden, God lectures peripatetic,
yet note how the orchids observe *otium sanctum*.

Listing of Photographs

1. Male lion's head [Jesus, Lion of Judah]
2. Merced River at Yosemite Valley [The Spring Rain]
3. Country house, Peacham, Vermont [Sleep Comes Gently]
4. Thaw on snow-covered lake [Late Winter's Thaw]
5. Vermont farm through rain-spattered window [The Rainy Season]
6. Island of trees in fog [Fog]
7. Waterfall among rocks [To a Waterfall]
8. Woman walking near lone tree [Calling Upon the Wind]
9. Railroad tracks stretching across high plains [The Interminable Tedium of the High Plains]
10. Cacti and nearby peak [The Desert as City]
11. Boardwalk and umbrellas at beach [The Shore]
12. Crab's claw and shell [At the Beach]
13. Rocky shore near Pebble Beach, California [Breakers]
14. Person in white amid the rocks [Island Prisons]
15. Fish in kelp forest [In the Turquoise Deserts of the Sea]
16. Hand holding dandelions [Carefree]
17. Close-up of light on flower [Upon Finding a Flower Blooming]
18. Wooden door and metal handles [The Lilies]
19. Water lily pads and flower reflection [Water-Lily Beauty]
20. Birds flying near building [Tumbling Nests]

Listing of Photographs

21. Haystacks, horses and wagon [Broadcast, Don't Drill]
22. Metal sculptures of wheat [Bumper Ennui]
23. Young girl near fruit stand [The Dangling Tomatoes]
24. Top-down view of pumpkin [Pumpkins and Gourds]
25. Woman's hands near blinds [Ungovernable Fingers]
26. Corn tassels [The Corn Palace]
27. Masks in store window [These Damnable Flies]
28. Head of a stag on the wall [The Prey]
29. Alert cat holding its paw [For Fluffy]
30. Mallard resting among grasses [The Animal Game]
31. Eggs set out in basket [Breakthrough]
32. Boy running toward church steeples [Hope]
33. Bearded fellow with bone and dogs [Congratulatory Feedback]
34. Two rhinoceroses together [Noah and the Ark]
35. Streaks of light above winter trees [An Imaginative Exercise for William James]
36. Tree and branches near dam [The Flood of Time]
37. Hand holding model Unisphere [A Utopian Solution]
38. Field of Brown-eyed Susans [The World's the Bride]
39. Silhouette of El Capitan [Thoughts of Human Grandeur]
40. Fish and reflection in aquarium [Creation Groans On]
41. Sow with piglets [Bless the Lord]
42. Two nuns in the Cloisters [Chewable Spirituality]
43. Sheep looking through fence [God Wants Only Lambs]
44. Trees with fall colors [A Morbid Autumn]
45. Wooden cross and flowers [Tumble-Down Crosses]
46. Donkey with head through fence [I'll Be Transformed]
47. Metropolitan Life Insurance tower clock [Absolute Zero]
48. Vine climbing up tree near wall [Death like a Vine]

Listing of Photographs

49. Fall leaves against dark background [Unbelief]
50. Woman on picnic bench near lake [The Hidden Things of God]
51. Rocks on sandy beach [Incalculable Things]
52. Hand reflected in glasses [Maya]
53. Virgin and child icon [Space . . .]
54. Female shadow on building [The Shadow]
55. Statue of doe and fawn [Time, That Fleeting Deer]
56. Someone gathering along rocky coast [On Gathering Stars]
57. Woman ascending in hot air balloon [Signs of the Zodiac]
58. Teepees on the high plains [Song of a Shaman]
59. Three people in canoe [How Do You Wake Up?]
60. Sunset on lake [Sunset]

Works Cited

Aesop. *Aesop's Fables*. Translated by Laura Gibbs. New York: Oxford University Press, 2002.
Aldington, Richard, ed. *The Viking Book of Poetry of the English-Speaking World, Volume Two*. New York: Viking, 1958.
Baker, John Austin. *Travels in Oudamovia*. Leighton Buzzard, UK: Faith Press, 1976.
Baum, L. Frank. *The Wizard of Oz*. New York: Award Book, n.d.
Biedermann, Hans. *Dictionary of Symbolism*. Translated by James Hulbert. New York: Facts on File, 1992.
Bonaventure. *The Soul's Journey into God, The Tree of Life, The Life of St. Francis*. Translated by Ewert Cousins. New York: Paulist, 1978.
Bulgakov, Sergius. *A Bulgakov Anthology*. Edited by James Pain and Nicholas Zernov. Philadelphia: Westminster, 1976.
Cahalane, Victor H. "Lion." In *The World Book Encyclopedia, Volume 11*, 298–301. Chicago: Field Enterprises Educational Corporation, 1960.
Catholic Church. *Catechism of the Catholic Church*. San Francisco: Ignatius, 1994.
Charbonneau-Lassay, Louis. *The Bestiary of Christ*. Translated and abridged by D. M. Dooling. New York: Arkana, 1992.
Chesterton, G. K. *The Penguin Complete Father Brown*. New York: Penguin, 1981.
Endicott, Norman J., ed. *The Prose of Sir Thomas Browne*. New York: Norton, 1972.
Ford, Paul F. *Companion to Narnia*. New York: HarperCollins, 1994.
Frye, Northrop, ed. *Selected Poetry and Prose of William Blake*. New York: Modern Library, 1953.
Hahn, Samuel J. *Learning from the Lizard: Bible Animal Object Lessons*. Lima, OH: CSS Publishing, 2000.
James, William. *The Will to Believe and Other Essays in Popular Philosophy and Human Immortality*. New York: Dover, 1956.
Kerr, Hugh T., and John M. Mulder, eds. *Conversions: The Christian Experience*. Grand Rapids: Eerdmans, 1983.
Lane, Belden C. *Ravished by Beauty: The Surprising Legacy of Reformed Spirituality*. New York: Oxford University Press, 2011.
Lewis, C. S. *The Lion, the Witch, and the Wardrobe*. New York: Macmillan, 1953.
———. *Surprised by Joy: The Shape of My Early Life*. London: HarperCollins, 1977.
Linzey, Andrew. *Animal Theology*. Urbana, IL: University of Illinois Press, 1995.
Lofting, Hugh. *The Story of Doctor Dolittle*. New York: Dell, 1967.

Works Cited

Mandeleker, Amy and Elizabeth Powers, eds. *Pilgrim Souls: A Collection of Spiritual Autobiographies*. New York: Simon & Schuster, 1999.

McDermott, Gerald R. *Everyday Glory: The Revelation of God in All Reality*. Grand Rapids: Baker, 2018.

McGrath, Alister E., ed. *Theology: The Basic Readings*. Malden, MA: Blackwell, 2008.

McKim, Donald K. *The Westminster Dictionary of Theological Terms, Second Edition Revised and Expanded*. Louisville: Westminster John Knox, 2014.

McNeill, John T., ed. *Calvin: Institutes of the Christian Religion, Volume 1*. Translated by Ford Lewis Battles. Philadelphia: Westminster Press, 1960.

McVey, Kathleen E., trans. *Ephrem the Syrian: Hymns*. Mahwah, NJ: Paulist, 1989.

Nash, James A. *Loving Nature: Ecological Integrity and Christian Responsibility*. Nashville: Abingdon, 1991.

Olin, John C., ed. *The Autobiography of St. Ignatius Loyola: With Related Documents*. Translated by Joseph F. O'Callaghan. New York: Harper & Row, 1974.

Outler, Albert, C., ed. *The Works of John Wesley, Volume 2, Sermons II: 34–70*. Nashville: Abingdon, 1985.

Pliny the Elder. *Natural History: A Selection*. Translated by John F. Healey. New York: Penguin, 1991.

Reade, Julian Edgeworth. "The Assyrian Royal Hunt." In *I Am Ashurbanipal, King of the World, King of Assyria*, edited by Gareth Brereton, 52–79. New York: Thames & Hudson, 2018.

Ryken, Leland, et al., eds. "Lion." In *Dictionary of Biblical Imagery*, 514–15. Downers Grove, IL: InterVarsity, 1998.

Sandburg, Carl. *Harvest Poems: 1910–1960*. New York: Harcourt Brace Jovanovich, 1960.

Sayers, Dorothy. *Letters to a Diminished Church: Passionate Arguments for the Relevance of Christian Doctrine*. Nashville: W Publishing, 2004.

Schaller, George B. *Golden Shadows, Flying Hooves*. Chicago: University of Chicago Press, 1983.

Smith, John E., et al., eds. *A Jonathan Edwards Reader*. New Haven, CT: Yale University Press, 1995.

Spurgeon, C. H. *C. H. Spurgeon's Autobiography, Volume 1: 1834–1854*. Compiled by his wife. Chicago: Curts & Jennings, 1898.

St. Therese of Lisieux. *The Autobiography of St. Therese of Lisieux: The Story of a Soul*. Translated by John Beevers. Garden City, NY: Image, 1957.

Sullivan, Walter. *We Are Not Alone: The Search for Intelligent Life on Other Worlds, Revised Edition*. New York: McGraw-Hill, 1966.

Thoreau, Henry David. *Excursions*. Edited by Joseph J. Moldenhauer. Princeton: Princeton University Press, 2007.

Underhill, Evelyn. *Mysticism: A Study in the Nature and Development of Man's Spiritual Consciousness*. New York: New American Library, 1955.

White, Gilbert. *The Natural History of Selbourne*. Edited by Richard Mabey. New York: Penguin, 1977.

White, T. H., trans. and ed. *The Book of Beasts*. New York: Dover, 2013.

www.ingramcontent.com/pod-product-compliance
Lightning Source LLC
Chambersburg PA
CBHW070702100426
42735CB00039B/2440